D1566015

THE HERO LEADER

WHY EFFECTIVE LEADERS COMBINE
STRENGTHS AND WEAKNESSES

dr. stephen r. graves

dr. stephen r. graves
The Hero Leader
Published by KJK Inc. Publishing
P.O. Box 9448
Fayetteville, AR 72702

Details in some anecdotes and stories have been changed to protect the identities of the persons involved.

ISBN [[978-1-940794-12-9]]

Steve is dedicated to drive conversations, uncover insights, and publish around four themes he is passionate about: Leadership Development, Social Innovation, Practical Faith, and Organizational Strategy.

For more resources from KJK Publishing and to view Steve's blog visit www.stephenrgraves.com

THE HERO LEADER
WHY EFFECTIVE LEADERS COMBINE
STRENGTHS AND WEAKNESSES

THE POWER
OF AND

*A Call to Rethink
Strength-Driven Leadership*

WE LIVE IN an either/or world. It's a world of extremes, of pendulum swings where innovation is nothing more than offering a "one up" on the competition. In the leadership world the concept of "leading from your strengths" continues to drive the pace. But have you ever wondered what was there before the strengths finder? What did good leadership look like before we all started leading from our strengths? Was being a leader always a matter of being *either* a great visionary *or* a great administrator?

What happened to the leader who knew how to inspire *and* instruct, who could innovate *and* get involved, who could get their hands dirty with the daily grind while their heart soared miles away dreaming of what could be?

There was a time when leaders didn't just focus on what they were good at; they focused on being a *complete* leader.

If they found a deficiency, they worked on it, which is part of becoming a well-rounded person *and* leader.

It's not whether you are a visionary *or* an administrator, it's that you work on being both. It's possible to be competent in administration while leading from the comfort of your visionary strength. It's possible to enjoy a dynamic career linking what you are excellent at with what you are competent in. The two are not mutually exclusive.

We like to think of leadership in terms of effectiveness. To be a great leader, we say, you must be effective, and to be effective you should find your strengths. But what do we really mean by "effectiveness"? And isn't a leader more than the sum total of his or her strengths?

When you think of leadership, do you think of it only in terms of what a person can help an organization accomplish? Or do you think about a leader in qualitative terms? The great leaders are the ones we're still following, still quoting, still modeling our own path after. They possess a *quality* to which we aspire.

In his seminal work *Leadership Is An Art*[1], Max Depree says, "Leaders owe a covenant to the organization or institution, which is, after all, a group of people. Leaders owe the organization a new reference point for what caring, purposeful, committed people can be in the institutional setting."

The qualitative view of what a true leader should be cannot come from a one-dimensional leader, a leader who only focuses on honing their strengths. Rather, it must come from a leader who sees the big picture and understands that he or she has a primary role to play in creating this kind of environment.

Depree is not talking about a visionary, he's talking about a person—one who is multifaceted, one who understands that if they want to leave a legacy they need to be dialed into more than just their own talents. They need to be dialed into others.

EFFICIENT OR EFFECTIVE?

Our culture leans toward a "me-first" mentality when it comes to ambition and success.

It stands to reason that it would also imply a "me-centered" version of leadership. Typical leadership books largely focus on how to improve the self. You will be most effective if you constantly improve your skill set, if you *do things right*, if you do things the best.

But can you be truly *effective* if you only focus on ways to make yourself better? Strengths are important to leadership, but true leadership isn't measured by how well you perform *per se*. Rather, it is measured by how well it induces legacy. What is legacy if not the representative lives who follow you, who model your methods and carry on your work ethic?

"EFFICIENCY IS DOING THE
THING RIGHT. EFFECTIVENESS IS
DOING THE RIGHT THING."
–PETER DRUCKER

"The signs of outstanding leadership," says Depree, "appear primarily among the followers."

I think, in our quest to achieve, we have mistaken *efficiency* for *effectiveness.*

Operating from your strengths will certainly enable you to do things right, to be efficient. But, as Peter Drucker points out, *effective leadership* does the right thing. Here, Drucker is implying that the very nature of effectiveness is relational. We are effective leaders when we empower others to reach their own potential—that's the right thing to do. We are effective leaders when we operate from a state of wholeness—that's the right thing to pursue. Sure, as leaders we get things done right; that's paramount. But the things getting done are the *right* things.

Is it right to simply lead from my strengths and let other specialists pick up the pieces?

No. Rather, it is right to lead in a way that understands the value of seeking and achieving wholeness. Depree talks about this kind of leadership as an art form. I think he's on to something.

Art does not come easily and it certainly is not formed with a limited amount of materials. Oil paintings, poems, orchestral masterpieces all result from layered physical work, the inner experience of the artist as well as the rules that govern the particular artistic discipline.

Leadership, though not a form of high art, does demand that its participants master physical abilities, relate to people within organizations, and adhere to a certain ethic. An effective artist is able to evoke visceral reactions with a unified artistic expression. You don't see what goes into the painting, just the finished product.

Likewise, an effective leader should be able to point to the brilliance of a legacy that, though it was built with a certain level of efficiency, reveals unity born of complexity—i.e., a man or woman who made it their work to juggle several skill sets for the sake of relational effectiveness.

THE END OF PENDULUMS

I think the pendulums need to be broken. Our goal as leaders should be to adapt our efficiencies to the times while maintaining the disciplines that rise above trends.

You will always need to relate to people; you can't just sit in a white tower and innovate. You will always need to use your head and your heart. Just because you aren't a compassionate leader now doesn't mean you can't learn what it is to be compassionate and develop the qualities of tenderness and kindness.

Today, we need a leadership reset more than ever. Perhaps we need to return to a time when it was commonplace to pursue excellence in more than one discipline. When I think of my favorite do-it-all types, my mind jumps to the superhero world. Don't worry; I'm not suggesting that we, as leaders, should pursue fantastical skill sets or superhuman qualities. But I do think that we can learn a thing or two from a certain caped crusader.

SECTION 1

A NEW KIND OF LEADERSHIP HERO

CHAPTER 1

BASE JUMPING OFF SKYSCRAPERS

*Leadership Guidance from
the Dark Knight*

WHEN I WAS a kid, one of my heroes was Batman. I read Batman comic books until the pages came apart. Every Saturday morning I raced into the living room to watch cartoons and to see Batman save Gotham City from the evil schemes of the wily Joker. Batman always beat The Joker the same way: with the "WHAM! BAM! KAPOW!" of his black-gloved bat-fists.

Batman duked it out with the best of them, and, unlike most other superheroes, he did it without any superpowers—no X-ray vision, no superhuman strength, no spider webs, no swimming like a dolphin or flying like an eagle. Instead, he got by on his work ethic, wit, intelligence, and technology.

Batman was and is the ultimate Renaissance Man. He knows how to fly an airplane. He's an expert driver, regardless of the vehicle type or its horsepower. He knows chemistry, finance, biology, physics, history, art, and literature. He's a speed-reader with a photographic memory.

His intuition works better than a million-dollar alarm system, and his moral compass always points toward right over wrong.

And if he can't outwit his opponents or beat them with his gadgets, he can always fall back on his expertise in the martial arts. "WHAM! BAM! KAPOW!"

On the surface, it appears Batman somehow manages to achieve the impossible: being omni-competent. He stares down one of life's greatest enemies, with the unrelenting pressure to be all, know all, and do all—without flinching.

We idolize Batman because he was somehow able to be all things to all people. In Christopher Nolan's most recent interpretation of the shadowy figure, we find a billionaire philanthropist playboy who masquerades as a caped crusader—defeating the bad guys with wit, technology, and determination. He can BASE jump off skyscrapers, develop new weaponry, and execute his vision for justice. We all want to be that type of leader.

But we quickly realize that we can't be experts in six disparate disciplines. And yet, the shrinking corporate landscape demands more and more from its executives.

Leaders in the twenty-first century understand all too well the pressure to be all, know all, and do all. We understand that what "got us here" might not "keep us here," because we know that "new" and "different" reign supreme, and for good reason.

We know last year's results sit in the archives. So we glance into the superhero mirror and yearn for more tricks, tips, and tools. And staring back at us are two conflicting realities: 1) the things we don't do well might cost us our jobs, and 2) we will never do everything equally well.

We hold our breath and hope we can reinvent ourselves like Batman does in each new movie. Only we don't have brilliant directors scripting our every move. The responsibility to grow, to develop, and to discover the appropriate leadership qualities rests squarely on our shoulders.

"EFFECTIVE LEADERSHIP IS
NOT ABOUT MAKING SPEECHES
OR BEING LIKED; LEADERSHIP
IS DEFINED BY RESULTS NOT
ATTRIBUTES." –PETER DRUCKER

CHAPTER 2

DUELING REALITIES

*Escaping the Pigeonhole that
Padlocks Your Potential*

THE FIFTEENTH CENTURY'S Renaissance Humanism movement began as Italian do-it-alls, or as Leon Battista Alberti suggested, "A man can do all things if he but wills them." Believing man to be the center of the universe, it was natural to chase "all knowledge" in pursuit of becoming what the Greeks called a "polymath"—or, if you prefer the Latin, "*Homo Universalis*" (a universal man).

A gentleman living in the Renaissance era was expected to speak multiple languages, play a musical instrument, and even write a bit of poetry. The idea of the universal person stemmed from an approach to education that did not specialize in single subjects. Rather, it spanned science, philosophy, and theology.

To attend *university*—a term that was coined in this era—was to attain broad expertise, to become a well-versed citizen, and to maintain the idea that the human person can and *should* seek to master several fields.

But the idea that someone can obtain ultimate polymath success like a Michelangelo or Francis Bacon is ridiculous. No one can be brilliant at everything. We can, however, strive for the Renaissance ideal of gaining a broad knowledge base.

What can the modern business leader learn from the polymath? How would you react to a *Fast Company* cover story titled: "The Drive to be the Omni-Competent Leader"?

You might respond like many in today's business world who claim that being a specialist is the most effective way to lead. A common theme among management and leadership gurus tells us to find our strength and not waste time becoming something we're not.

Why dabble in poetry since you're no Wordsworth? Who cares about science since you need only concern yourself with the bottom line, right? After all, you can hire or outsource to compensate for your weaknesses. Be a specialist; pick an area to be great at, and go after it full throttle.

Furthermore, as leaders, we should identify and cultivate the strengths of our direct reports rather than their weaknesses.

Lord Colin Sharman, chairman of Aegis Group, put it this way: "A weakness is there: it's something you have to take into account, but the way in which you get superior performance out of a group of people is to figure out what they're good at and then get them into a role that uses that to the maximum advantage." [2]

This advice carries merit. But eventually an unrelenting adversary punches it hard in the face: *Reality*.

Only focusing on what you're good at and only highlighting your strengths does not work in the diverse demands of today's integrated and competitive world. As Batman learned, it won't sustain a career—not in Gotham City, not in the toy stores, and not in the dog-eat-dog streets of the modern marketplace.

The "strengths" approach presents a great danger for leaders because it pigeonholes them in ways that padlock their potential. And they typically never see the jailer coming. It's the classic example of a glass ceiling, one they can't see and can't break through. They advanced in the earlier stages of their careers precisely because they were accomplished in a few specific and related skill sets. It worked then, so why fix it now?

As they rose into positions of greater influence, these leaders would tell themselves, "Oh, I may not be much of a manager, but where I really excel is at the big picture of vision." Or, "True, I don't do a good job of administration, but boy, can I sell." Or, "OK, so what if I am a jerk? I know how to make people get things done, don't I?"

> **"OUR CHIEF WANT IS SOMEONE WHO WILL INSPIRE US TO BE WHAT WE KNOW WE COULD BE."**
> **– RALPH WALDO EMERSON**

They would excuse themselves from their weaknesses by spotlighting their strengths. But their singular focus developed blind spots—blind spots that can send the best of careers into a ditch.

There are two things wrong with this whole line of thinking. First, focusing on strengths tends to work on your *personal efficiency*. As I said earlier, personal efficiency is a great tool to possess on your leadership tool belt. But it's not the only tool. You can't build a house with just a hammer and nails. You need more tools, more skill sets. You can be the fastest nail-hammering carpenter in the world and still not be able to build a house. I want you to be efficient and to do things right. But even more than that, I want you to be an effective leader who works at developing a quality tool belt.

Second, focusing on strengths misses the point of effective leadership. If you want to be a top-tier leader, you must develop personal wholeness that focuses on how you can empower and equip others to reach their potential.

If you do nothing but hone your own strengths, at some point you'll discover a serious lack in your ability to lead others well.

THE END OF ONE-TRICK PONIES

There was a time in American history when entrepreneurs put together small traveling shows featuring trained animals—dancing bears, dogs that could walk on a ball, horses that could stand on an upside-down bucket. Such tricks played well with audiences, the *first time* they saw them.

The smart circus ringmaster recognized this and knew he wouldn't last long with a cast of one-trick ponies. The ponies must either learn something new or the show would be forced out of town. After more than 25 years of coaching effective leaders, it's clear to me the shelf life has expired on one-trick executive ponies.

The modern title for these folks is "the executive specialist"—corporate leaders who excel at certain aspects of leading and/or managing while ignoring other essential aspects. Industrialization brought a trend toward specialization, but look around you today. A knowledge-based workforce grows. And in tight labor markets where companies try to do more with less, multitalented leaders will be in high demand.

Consider the NFL quarterback. Teams long for an athletic quarterback, but that won't get you far if you don't have a strong and accurate arm. Oh, and you'd better be able to master the playbook, not to mention having the intuition that tells you when to run out of the pocket before that 280-pound defensive end plants you facemask-first into the turf. You also better cultivate a good relationship with the owner, the head coach, the temperamental star receiver, the other players, and the media, while avoiding any sort of personal crisis that might sack your reputation. If you rely solely on your physical abilities you won't last long in professional football.

The elite quarterbacks in the NFL are the quarterbacks who master the physical and mental aspects of the game.

Batman knew it. Deep, lasting success requires a wide repertoire of qualities both professional and personal.

Today's business landscape, in fact, demands multi-functionality at almost every level. The executive specialist, therefore, is out of a job: his resume, too lean. His capabilities, too few. The challenges he faces, too diverse; his opportunities, too unpredictable; his limitations, too glaring. His bandwidth of contribution to the company is too narrow to justify the high cost of keeping him, or at the very least, the cost of advancing him. He's no longer a superhero; he's just another guy in a suit (hopefully not spandex with a mask).

This harsh reality for the executive specialist creates an unrelenting pressure to achieve something that's not feasible: *excellence at everything*. The idea that we can be instinctively great at everything and be all things to all people is impossible. It's a mindset perpetuated by the self-help industry.

Most self-help gurus teach from a silo, focusing only on the area they consider their expertise—fatherhood, salesmanship, listening, investing, real estate, team-building, cooking, dieting, and on and on goes the list. They establish an ideal for greatness in a particular area and sell the idea that anyone can obtain it.

While many of these gurus are well intentioned and offer

worthy advice, many propagate the misguided notion that the key to omni-competence is simply attending omni-seminars.

Could you excel at any one of those areas? Probably so. But could you excel at all of them at the same time? Not a chance.

Every single leader I know is juggling a number of balls all at the same time. Why? Because life and work require your participation and competence in a number of areas, not just the things you excel at.

We all wear a number of hats every day, all at the same time—boss, employee, partner, donor, father, son, neighbor, board member, coach, or owner. Success requires us to be more than just one dimension of greatness.

So these dueling realities—1) Omni-competence is impossible, and 2) What you can't do will be your downfall—create the modern executive's greatest challenge: *how to effectively deal with the unrelenting pressure to be all, know all, and do all.*

Because while becoming a polymath like da Vinci is impossible, we still must strive for the Renaissance ideal—being well rounded. We can't afford to ignore the areas that don't come naturally to us. When it comes to executive qualities, we need the good *and* the great … not just the great.

We can avoid this challenge and commit ourselves to a course toward mediocrity. Or we can embrace it, knowing that we'll never achieve perfection, but that we can prevent our weaknesses from becoming career-fatal liabilities.

"WHEN IT COMES TO
EXECUTIVE QUALITIES,
WE NEED THE GOOD AND
THE GREAT ... NOT JUST
THE GREAT."

CHAPTER 3

MY SOLUTION BOX

*Qualities Every Leader Needs
to Discover And Develop*

IN MY LEADERSHIP coaching practice I often offer a "CEO tour" in which I guide clients on a short pilgrimage of prearranged meetings to glean the insights of a select group of top-floor corporate leaders. With one young rising executive, for instance, I arranged a three-day tour with five CEOs in the Midwest, and the many issues we discussed included the area of hiring, motivating, and retaining top-level employees.

One question we posed to each CEO was, "What traits are you looking for when you're hiring senior leaders?" An interesting picture emerged from our various conversations. They weren't necessarily looking for that natural-born genius whose awe-inspiring talent eclipsed all the rest. Yes, they wanted talent, but just as important was a broad collective of leadership qualities.

The conclusion was that leaders often must work on rounding out their born-with-it gifting by developing new capacities that come through intentional, focused discipline learning.

In other words, we all have competencies to be *discovered* as well as competencies to be *developed*.

Over the last few years I have compiled a list of capabilities required to lead at the top, in the middle, or on your way up from the bottom of any healthy organization.

The more I have pondered these qualities, the more I've realized they are opposite sides of the same coin.

Harvey Two Face, one of Batman's many adversaries, would insist on flipping his coin, picking the option the coin gave to him, and turning a blind eye to the other. We have come to learn that in the movie there was only one coin and it had the same thing on both sides. But the qualities required of modern leaders in the modern world require more than the one answer. A more diverse solution box is required.

"NO ONE IS BORN EQUALLY
CAPABLE ON BOTH SIDES.
WE ARE HARDWIRED
TOWARD ONE SIDE IN EACH
SET, AND THAT'S OK."

I have identified seven sets of qualities. The pairings hinge on the beauty and power of the *AND*, not the *OR*. I think of them as the paradoxical parallels of modern leadership. But for our purposes here, let's call them "The Seven Collective Qualities of a Leader."

No one is born equally capable on both sides. We are hardwired toward one side in each set, and that's OK. The market, however, requires that we develop at least conscious competence in all of these areas of effective leadership, even if it doesn't come naturally. We can staff to our weaknesses, but, at the same time, it's imperative that we make every effort to round out our own leadership skills. We cannot be content as an executive specialist.

Read through the "The Seven Collective Qualities of a Leader" and tag the side of the tandem in which you are strongest. You also might arrange them in order of what comes naturally versus what is outside your innate wiring.

Then mark the quality sets that seem to be especially critical to your current work assignment. Later, we'll examine each in greater depth.

1. Being Results Driven AND People Focused
2. Doing Friday's Payroll AND Inventing the Future
3. Having Heart AND Using Your Head
4. Thinking Corporately AND Working Functionally
5. Leading Others AND Managing Yourself
6. Feeling Confident AND Being Humble
7. Embracing Team AND Performing Alone

These quality sets require a learning process. Most of us fall somewhere within the bounds of a matrix commonly known as the Four Stages of Competence. This matrix, built on ideas that date back as far as Socrates and Confucius, helps us better grasp the concept of multidimensional talent.

Unconscious Incompetence	*Conscious Incompetence*
Conscious Competence	*Unconscious Competence*

Unconscious Incompetence – If you don't understand something or know how to do it and you don't recognize this deficit, then welcome to "unconscious incompetence," otherwise known as "you don't know what you don't know" or "blissful ignorance." By definition, you don't even know you're there but at least you aren't stressing out about it. Example: The tone-deaf American Idol contestant who thinks she can sing really well.

Conscious Incompetence – If you recognize that you're deficient in understanding an idea or carrying out a task, but you're not doing anything to address it, then welcome to "conscious incompetence." For example, you don't speak Russian. You know you don't speak Russian. You're making no effort to learn Russian. And if this becomes an issue, you'll hire a translator.

Conscious Competence – If you understand or know how to do a particular skill, but executing it requires focused concentration, then welcome to "conscious competence."

If you're great at something but it is more a product of discipline and hard work rather than innate wiring, you're

"YOU'VE GOT TO EAT WHILE
YOU DREAM. YOU'VE GOT TO
DELIVER ON SHORT-RANGE
COMMITMENTS, WHILE YOU
DEVELOP A LONG-RANGE
STRATEGY AND VISION AND
IMPLEMENT IT. THE SUCCESS
IS DOING BOTH. WALKING
AND CHEWING GUM IF YOU
WILL." – JACK WELCH

addressing "conscious competence." A golfer, for instance, wants to achieve "muscle memory" that allows him to repeat the perfect swing. Or for many of the non-artistic types, this reflects our ability to color within the lines. We can do it, but we have to really focus and the more we do it, the better we become.

Unconscious Competence – When we hear someone say, "He or she was born to do that," you are witnessing the assertion of "unconscious competence." If you've mastered a skill or concept so thoroughly that it's become second nature and you can perform it without concentrating too deeply, then welcome to "unconscious competence." There are many examples, but let's start with preparing a bowl of ice cream for a late night snack. Some of us can do that with our eyes closed.

But this muscle is not restricted to hobbies and pastime activities. Most people have a skill or two vital to their work that is second nature to them. Most of us had at least one teacher in our educational journey that we would say was "born to teach."

We usually use that term to heap verbal accolades on the Michael Jordan's of the world (at the time of this printing we are still waiting for the undisputed heir to his throne).

However, I would argue that every average Joe also has at least one "unconscious competence" skill set. It might not achieve front-page status, but it is there nonetheless.

Understanding these stages and where we fall on the grid provides us with a starting point as we strive toward greater balance in our competence as a leader. We can assess and evaluate, then make a plan and work the plan so that we can achieve positive movement within this grid when it comes to the Seven Collective Qualities of a Leader.

Every aspiring leader—not some or most, but every single one—should set a minimum standard of "conscious competence" when it comes to these 14 areas of leadership skills. Why? Not because they are the latest version of a leadership hot list, but because they are essential to leading and managing the everyday affairs of any healthy enterprise.

SECTION 2

THE SEVEN COLLECTIVE QUALITIES OF THE HERO LEADER

CHAPTER 4

THE RELATABLE PRODUCER

Being Results Driven **AND** *People Focused*

AS EARLY AS the mid-1960s, Peter Drucker forecasted the dominant role of the knowledge worker in the global economy, and that once-emerging trend eventually became an established reality.

"The most valuable assets of a 20th-century company were its production equipment," Drucker wrote in 1999. "The most valuable asset of a 21st-century institution, whether business or non-business, will be its knowledge workers and their productivity." [3]

His 1992 prediction that managing the productivity of those workers would be "the biggest and toughest challenge facing managers in the developed countries for decades to come" has also held true, perhaps even more than even he expected.

Conventional wisdom holds that you are either a chatty people person or a task-driven maniac, but in actuality you cannot afford to neglect either side of the pendulum. Like I said before, let's break all the pendulums! You may be stronger in one, but you need proficiency in both if you hope to stand any chance of successfully leading a modern workforce driven largely by knowledge workers.

In *The World Is Flat*, Thomas L. Friedman explains that delivering results against goals is imperative for economic survival in a time in which global competition is squeezing margins. Gone are the days when corporate payrolls had the luxury of fat workforces with departments that got anything they wanted.

The cost of labor is the Achilles' heel of American business. It is more expensive for an American to do something than it is for someone in India to do the same thing. That means we all must deliver more value per hour if we want to keep making a living. This new flattened world means that every position on the organizational chart must justify its existence every day. Results aren't optional if you want next month's paycheck. The company's bottom line is now your bottom line and my bottom line. There is no insulation from the reality of the market or its rigorous competitive demands.

At first glance, all of this might seem like a mandate for the taskmaster leader who can push workers with a singular focus on productivity because, after all, there are plenty of qualified applicants waiting for the next dissatisfied worker's job. But the high cost of turnover is one of several factors that make such an approach a risky proposition.

But that is only one side of the coin.

RELATE, RELATE, RELATE

The shift by the American workforce toward free agency brings with it a tremendous need for developing and/or upgrading your Relational Quotient (RQ). Since people know you are making no promises about their future, how you treat them matters all the more. No matter where you are in the pecking order, you cannot get where you need to go without the help of other stakeholders.

You need people.

And always remember, the larger your vision the bigger your people pool will have to be. Indeed, people have become their own bottom line, and you neglect them to your peril. Upgrading your personal and/or corporate RQ is a practical way to grow the human capital underneath your bottom line.

Furthermore, post-boomer generations simply will not put up with the old ways of working. They demand a work culture where relationships and people are shown respect. Who they work with is as important to them as what they do. The same

"CONVENTIONAL WISDOM HOLDS THAT YOU ARE EITHER A CHATTY PEOPLE PERSON OR A TASK-DRIVEN MANIAC, BUT IN ACTUALITY YOU CANNOT AFFORD TO NEGLECT EITHER SIDE OF THE PENDULUM."

goes for customers and vendors. It is one huge symbiotic web of relational links. With price squeezed to the max, decisions increasingly come down to relationships built on integrity and trust.

Your relational reliability largely determines the willingness of employees, vendors, and customers to join with you and stay with you.

Businesses increasingly face the same predicament of volunteer service organizations: Association is *voluntary*. So you have to learn to be the kind of person you need others to be for you. The Office Jerk is an endangered species. The Taskmaster must now lead with a velvet hammer. The Hatchet Man who delivers over everybody else's dead body will come calling the second time only to find that no one returns his call.

The double-edged truth is that both people and the bottom line matter. We know they are inextricably knotted together. When results matter, you have to know how to get other people to help you make results happen. That requires both task focus and people proficiency.

"YOU MANAGE THINGS; YOU
LEAD PEOPLE."
—REAR ADMIRAL GRACE
MURRAY HOPPER

BEING RESULTS DRIVEN AND PEOPLE FOCUSED

☑ TRUE ☐ FALSE

RESULTS DRIVEN

☐ ☐   The people I lead have clear goals and performance metrics they are measured against.

☐ ☐   My goals are known by everyone on my team and don't "move" all the time.

☐ ☐   I am willing to hold under-performers accountable.

☐ ☐   I generally over-deliver on my results when given a task.

☐ ☐   I easily say NO to assignments or requests that I know are unreasonable or that I can't accomplish.

PEOPLE FOCUSED

☐ ☐   I regularly show gratitude and
appreciation to those I lead.

☐ ☐   I listen. People feel heard and understood
by me.

☐ ☐   The people I lead love the culture we
have created.

☐ ☐   Ongoing conversations with people on
my team energize me.

☐ ☐   I have a good knowledge of the
emotional and mental state of the people
reporting to me.

☐ ☐   I am known for my energy and warmth
toward people.

CHAPTER 5

THE FUTURE
LOOKS GREASY

Doing Friday's Payroll **AND**
Inventing the Future

THERE ARE TWO key horizontal elements to any enterprise production: Creating future opportunity and delivering on yesterday's promises. One focuses forward; the other keeps a watch backwards. One is about the windshield; the other is about the rearview mirror. The tendency is to either be a visionary or be a deliverer. If you're involved in leadership today, however, you must develop competence in both inventing the future of tomorrow and delivering on the Friday's payroll of yesterday.

Tomorrow is a blank piece of paper. Do nothing and that's what it remains: Blank. It has to be written. You have to create your opportunities. You have to constantly reinvent the future, for yourself and for your company. Evolve or die. It is that simple.

One of the new "C-Suite" titles showing up more and more is the CI—the Chief Innovator (might be called a different term but the same idea).

Once upon a time, the products and services that came from innovative ideas became ingrained in societies for centuries with only modest modifications. There weren't many ways to improve a plow until you could hook it to a tractor instead of to animals.

In today's marketplace, however, success is like bread. It has a short shelf life, so you'd better be making the next new batch, now. And next year's version better be "new and improved" or even totally remade.

Innovation applies to products and services, as well as to business models and management styles. If you produce it, sell it, use it, encounter it, or step in it, chances are it's changing around you and you must change with it—or better yet, become the agent of the next significant change.

Those who most need improvement with the discipline

of inventing the future—the operational implementers—are typically strong on consistent administration and operational maintenance, but you can bet your pet pooch that their future vision is underdeveloped. Engineering the future is a discipline as well as a gift. It requires regular time invested in thinking ahead. If your five-year plan is more than a year old, then you are already behind on the future.

A senior executive of a large public company recently said to me, "Every company I know in every industry you can think of is in course correction mode. It seems we are relooking at our strategic plan every six to twelve months."

Give yourself a quick invent-the-future checkup.

+ What dreams never seem to move forward from year to year?
+ How long has it been since you had a new "vision" for your job or the company?
+ What's the last seminar or training event you attended that really helped you sharpen your saw?

You cannot afford *not* to know how to reinvent your future. If thinking forward doesn't come naturally, then make it a scheduled discipline. You might need to block off an hour or two a week, perhaps more. A day away from the office to contemplate the future might be the one thing that saves you and your organization.

THE ART OF CLOUD WALKING

On the other hand, many leaders seldom lack for ideas about the future and even have a whole closet full of yesterday's ideas that never got anywhere. Thinking up something new is a no-brainer for many; the hard part is paying for what's already on order—it's doing Friday's payroll.

Friday's payroll represents all the things you have to do

"THERE IS NO POWER ON EARTH THAT CAN NEUTRALIZE THE INFLUENCE OF A HIGH, SIMPLE AND USEFUL LIFE."
–BOOKER T. WASHINGTON

today that fulfill past commitments. It is the running list that captures all the obligations, agreements, and pledges you have made that require resources today to fulfill them. In its most elementary example, it is a worker and boss agreeing at the first of the week on work and payment. If the worker works all week along certain guidelines, the boss will pay him on that Friday for that week's work. The boss has to make sure he has the resources to fulfill his Friday payroll promise. And by the way, most of the things on our daily to-do list are in this category.

How are you at delivering on yesterday's promises? Being a visionary by itself won't secure your future. Visionaries must tool themselves to follow through. Ideas are a dime a dozen.

Wanna Be's have tons of ideas. "The best plan," as Drucker put it, "is only good intentions." Those who succeed are those who know how to take an idea and actually make it happen.

Keeping payroll current is a discipline, and I'm not talking about cutting and mailing the checks. Those of us with our heads in the clouds have to schedule a regular descent to earth where we get dirty doing what it takes to make the future happen. The future happens today. If active implementation is not part of your today, then tomorrow never arrives.

If you don't develop the discipline of follow-through, the people who are under you get frustrated and burn out.

Soon you'll discover you aren't leading at all; you'll turn around and realize you're just going on a walk because no one is following you. They all quit because they got tired of picking up your dropped balls. People will stop trusting you. Ideas bank on the credibility of delivery. To the degree that you are known for making things happen, your ideas will find a greater listening.

So get out the *bills*, see what promises you owe—no matter how big or how small—and start *writing checks*.

"TO THE DEGREE THAT
YOU ARE KNOWN FOR
MAKING THINGS HAPPEN,
YOUR IDEAS WILL FIND A
GREATER LISTENING."

DOING FRIDAY'S PAYROLL *AND* INVENTING THE FUTURE

☑TRUE ☐ FALSE

FRIDAY'S PAYROLL

☐ ☐　　The work projects that I lead are on time and on budget.

☐ ☐　　I look for ways to improve efficiency.

☐ ☐　　I rarely have a bunch of undone things on my list from week to week.

☐ ☐　　My reports and team are regularly picking up dropped balls around me.

☐ ☐　　I have an intuitive sense on the state/progress of projects under my command.

INVENTING THE FUTURE

☐ ☐   Thinking forward usually energizes me.

☐ ☐   I have a vision for what I want our group to become five years from now.

☐ ☐   I have an intuitive sense of how to build the future.

☐ ☐   I love to doodle and dream about "the next big idea" for my company.

☐ ☐   I am known for being able to think around the corners.

☐ ☐   I am known for my energy and warmth toward people.

CHAPTER 6

NO MORE HEAD CASES

Having Heart **AND**
Using Your Head

ONE OF THE latest flavors of trendy leadership theory is the rise in popularity of "leading from the heart." The re-appreciation of a leader with a high EQ (Emotional Quotient) comes as a breath of fresh air after the long, oppressive days when it seemed like being a jerk was a prerequisite to promotion to the coveted title of Headstrong Business Tyrant. But there were reasons why the HBT rose to success—he or she was smart, focused, determined, and productive. And we still need their skills in the modern marketplace. Is it really possible to embody both skills?

I say yes.

The realization of the heart's importance to leadership, however, was a long overdue correction. The traditional choleric, task-driven approach to business was heavily dependent on a left-brain addiction to linear logic. In this incarnation, the essence of every business—it was thought—could be mapped on organizational charts and spreadsheets.

Maybe so, but such businesses had a massive blind spot: *Human capital or real people management.*

It took a generational shift to correct this imbalance. People who grew up with parents from the automation age simply did not buy it. They recognized the reality of the emperor's lack of clothes and did not mind saying so. They saw the life carnage of that world and refused to sign up. When they were old enough to start their own businesses and write their own business books, they wrote a very different story. They saw that every business transaction is actually a human interaction. They knew that not just our intellect, but that all of our senses are crucial to accurate perception and decision-making. They knew that we need to listen not just to reason, but to our gut, as well.

After the 2006 Sago, West Virginia, coal mine disaster—a

cave-in resulting in 12 deaths—the ABC news magazine *PrimeTime Live* interviewed Wilbur Ross, the then billionaire takeover mogul who owned the Sago mine. Ross squirmed under ABC's grilling questions about the safety of the mine and his complicity. To try and make the best of a PR disaster, Ross explained that his holding company had given $2 million to start a fund to help the families of the victims of the accident. Then ABC's reporter asked a question for which the heart would tell you there was only one right answer.

"Have you personally put any money in?"

It was a million dollar question for a man who'd made billions spotting troubled companies, buying them cheap, turning them around, and making huge profits. But all he could offer was a ten-cent answer.

"We own about a third of the company," he said, "and we will decide what to do about a personal contribution as we see what comes in from outside."[4]

Ross, a master at squeezing profit out of businesses that others discarded as worthless, had made an unforgivable mistake as a leader. In a time of human tragedy, he had not acted instinctively from his heart. He appeared far more concerned about "corporate chess moves" than about "personal concerns." Although his head seemed to be represented, his heart looked to be on vacation.

There are those of us left-brained leaders who still need tutoring in right-brain efficiency. If that's you, one of the easiest ways to increase your EQ, or heart-based leadership ability, is to constantly query those around you who are naturally your opposite. You need to see with the eyes of your heart before you can factor the left-brain logic of the world more effectively into your leadership maximization equation.

Empathy is a capability nurtured in both sides of the brain.

"LEADERSHIP IS A POTENT
COMBINATION OF STRATEGY
AND CHARACTER. BUT IF YOU
MUST BE WITHOUT ONE, BE
WITHOUT THE STRATEGY."
– NORMAN SCHWARZKOPF

With that said, there is no need to throw the baby out with the bath water. Business is not a séance session. Some of us need to come back to earth and deal with reality. A business that is all heart and no profit will be soon be empathetically hugging people as they go out the door just before the lights are turned off. If you aren't using your head, then don't be surprised when your heart finds itself in a world of hurt.

Much of business remains left-brain dependent, and it always will be. The bottom line is still the bottom line. Every business deal is a very complex series of chess moves that must be mapped on a moving board with multiple threats on all sides.

The more complex a business decision is, the more time and energy must be spent understanding every little detail and how each part fits into the whole. A smile and a handshake are helpful, but it's often the toilsome work spent behind the scenes that will likely determine the success of the project. You don't just want to feel good about a project; you want to *do good*.

Even the most careful sometimes are not careful enough. NASA is as left-brained as they come. Yet the 1986 explosion of the space shuttle Challenger just after takeoff exposed the tragic mistake that something had been missed. The culprit, they learned, was the faulty design of a simple O-ring gasket. The pre-launch planning had not been thorough enough.

It only takes one O-ring failure to blow any business apart. Business failures invariably can be traced back to overlooked flaws in the original plan or the daily execution.

Effective leaders constantly update their strategies and plans, evaluating and reevaluating the latest data shaping their businesses realities. At the same time, however, they don't do it in a vacuum that locks out emotions.

They understand the very real economic value of relationships and the harsh consequences that await an organization that neglects its human capital and its social responsibilities. They understand they have to take ownership of the decisions they make with their heads, and that they can't delegate leadership that comes from the heart. So they'd better get to work improving both.

*HAVING HEART **AND***
USING YOUR HEAD

☑ TRUE ☐ FALSE

HAVING HEART

☐☐   I trust my gut when making decisions.

☐☐   I am known for my strong connectivity and for building relationships.

☐☐   I am able to easily empathize with those I lead.

☐☐   Understanding the "situation" behind under-performers is important to me.

☐☐   I feel a moral responsibility to help those around me succeed.

USING YOUR HEAD

☐ ☐   I feel comfortable doing quantitative and qualitative analysis.

☐ ☐   I can set aside personal frustration in order to stay focused.

☐ ☐   I consider risk when I make significant decisions.

☐ ☐   I strongly believe one of the best gifts I give the people around me is to grow a "healthy and profitable" company, which insures long-term job opportunities.

☐ ☐   I enjoy monitoring the key gauges and metrics that drive my company's ongoing success.

CHAPTER 7

YOUR CANDY AND YOUR CONVEYOR BELT

Thinking Corporately **AND** *Working Functionally*

IN ONE OF the most famous episodes of *I Love Lucy*, the 1950s vintage comedy that's endured for decades in reruns, Lucy and Ethel get jobs in a candy factory. After failing in several departments, they are given one final chance—to wrap the chocolates. At first, they easily wrap the candies as they go by on a conveyor belt. But as the belt speeds up, they fall behind and frantically try to catch up. Knowing they'll get fired if "one piece" of candy makes it unwrapped to the next department, they lose focus and begin pulling the chocolate off the belt. Then, when they hear their boss coming, panic sets in and they hide the candy anywhere they can—in their hats, in their shirts, in their mouths.

Learn a lesson from Lucy: You have to keep an eye both on your candy and the conveyor belt. You have to do your own work at the same time you see it in the larger process of everything else headed in your direction. It should be no surprise that anticipation is always on the short list of qualities of effective leaders.

A balanced leader thinks both functionally and corporately. We all have to fulfill our function in the process. You've heard the saying, "too many cooks spoil the soup." That's because everyone wants to be a cook, but also someone needs to be a waiter and somebody has to be a supplier and somebody else needs to clean up and somebody else needs to organize all the ingredients and somebody else—you get the idea.

Find the roles that are yours, the ones that will slip through the cracks if you don't do them, and then do them. Do them well. Do them on time. Do them like they are supposed to be done.

The danger is working head down all the time, never looking up to see what's going on around us. Taking in the larger view means thinking corporately. We can't have a silo

"GREAT LEADERS ARE
ALMOST ALWAYS GREAT
SIMPLIFIERS, WHO
CAN CUT THROUGH
ARGUMENT, DEBATE,
AND DOUBT TO OFFER A
SOLUTION EVERYBODY CAN
UNDERSTAND."
–GENERAL COLIN POWELL

mentality. Business is an interconnected organism and we have to stay connected to its bigger picture to be effective at our small part of it.

This is one of the biggest challenges I see for rising leaders because it's so hard for them to shake free from the nose-to-the-grindstone approach that played such a key role in their initial advancements. Most mid-level leaders and upper managers are extremely competent within their vertical function. They are experts within their department, whether it's sales or marketing or accounting or production or technology or some other aspect of the business. They are the prototypical executive specialists.

The higher a person moves up within an organization, however, the greater the need to think corporately. The VP of sales has to know the key challenges facing the VP of creative services. The accounting department needs to understand the customer interfaces, and the local marketing team needs to be fully aware of the numbers and the accounting. Sure, some of this is achieved through cross training.

But it all starts with the premise that the higher up in the company, the greater the need for a corporate eye, not just functional hands.

In *E-Myth*, the classic look at how to beat the odds and build a small business that can survive, Michael Gerber points out that most people start their own business because they love a particular task. They are "technician owners"— they love to make pies or fix pipes or practice law.

To succeed over the long term, according to Gerber, the leader must also *manage* the business and *grow* the business. That means overseeing operations and finances, formulating goals, creating a vision and setting a plan, as well as, when appropriate, being the worker bee.

The emphasis becomes the word *executive* rather than the word *specialist*.

The same holds true in larger organizations. A CEO of a large public company called recently to ask if I'd coach him through this type of challenge. His board had requested that he retain a coach to help him learn how to work "*on* the business, not just *in* the business." He needed to develop his ability to collect and process the broader range of information he now needed for effective decision-making. In essence, he needed to think more corporately because he'd been promoted into a position that made seeing the big picture a non-negotiable.

Sometimes, decision-making gets challenged when we face functional decisions.

Sometimes, a corporate perspective helps us make better financial decisions, especially when competing resources are tight.

How many businesses have been sunk by someone "just doing his job / head down and only focused on one piece of the elephant without any regard for the bigger picture"? The captain of the RMS *Titanic* became obsessed with one goal.

He felt vertical pressure from the White Star Line for the new ship to break the transatlantic crossing record on its maiden voyage. That tunnel vision caused him to go faster than he ordinarily would have in an area with reported icebergs. When the lookout cried, "Ice dead ahead!" and he felt the scraping crunch against the hull, the more global picture of the ship's true situation flashed startlingly before him. But it was too late.

Every organizational captain needs to have both a clear focus on specific objectives and an unobstructed view of the 360-degree context. The key is to do *both*: To think corporately as you work functionally; to see down into the silo as well as all across the frontier.

THINKING CORPORATELY AND WORKING FUNCTIONALLY

☑ TRUE ☐ FALSE

THINING CORPORATELY

☐ ☐	I understand how other departments are impacted by one department's performance or decision.
☐ ☐	I am clear on what my value-add is to my organization as a whole.
☐ ☐	I don't have trouble staying high and strategic. In other words, I don't easily get pulled down into the verticals / silos / tactical details of day-to-day business.
☐ ☐	I have a clear grasp on the big picture and how all the moving parts fit together.
☐ ☐	I know what the overall critical success factors are that drive and deliver corporate success.

WORKING FUNCTIONALLY

☐ ☐   I correctly position the members of my team according to their strengths.

☐ ☐   I am not a bottleneck. People are not waiting on me to make decisions.
I stay on top of email and phone correspondence.

☐ ☐   I have a very high-performing team in my vertical or department.

☐ ☐   I can focus on "my assignment" and don't always have a wandering eye on other people's work and assignments. I can stay in my lane.

☐ ☐   I don't need to know how all the moving parts fit together. I live by the old adage, "Don't worry about the mule—just load the wagon."

CHAPTER 8

THE LION AND THE LEMMING

Leading Others **AND**
Managing Yourself

LEADERSHIP HAS AN inner and an outer dimension. Being a leader means both managing yourself and leading others. In talking about these topics, there are two animals that immediately come to mind—the lion and the lemming.

The lion leads a pride—the group of cats whose welfare he oversees. He makes sure they are fed. He takes the lead and sees that they get rest. He protects them from attack. He mediates the pecking order and keeps everyone in line. When a pride of lions has no leader, it faces an inner battle: Lions fighting each other for control. When there is a healthy leader at the top, the pride is at peace and can function and grow.

Leadership is like that at all levels. People need direction.

That direction includes input from below, but it's established from the top down. It is axiomatic that leaders have to lead. They have to take the initiative. They make it incumbent upon themselves to get the group from Point A to Point B. If the group is dysfunctional, then at some level it is always the leader's fault. Leaders own the bottom line, no matter how many people are involved with the variables.

Hurricane Katrina provided a classic case study in the breakdown of leadership. The failure to adequately respond to the 2005 disaster wasn't from the lack of a plan. The multi-million-dollar contingency study of a direct hurricane hit on New Orleans was sitting on the shelf in three-ring binders. It was not from the lack of resources. All the relief supplies were sitting in warehouses around the country. A fleet of buses was sitting in a parking lot in New Orleans. It was simply a problem of people not leading. The mayor of New Orleans did not take the lead in protecting his city with a rigorous evacuation. The director of FEMA did not take the initiative to act decisively once the problem was obvious. It was a comedy of errors caused by inaction.

No one acted like a lion and took the lead.

People and organizations need leadership.

There is a second type of animal, however, and this one makes a dangerous leader: The lemming.

Few of us have ever seen a live lemming and not many of us could pick one out of a *Wild Kingdom* photo lineup. You don't see lemmings in family crests or as the visual icons for movie studios. But these small rodents living in the Arctic Circle are famous in urban legend for following their leader in mass suicidal plunges off cliffs. The lemming leader is highly effective at moving his followers. The problem is that he is leading them to a steep fall onto unforgiving rocks. The lemming has no internal moral compass. He does not lead himself before he leads others. He steps out in a whimsical direction and takes others with him.

Enron was a case of a lemming leadership disaster. Misguided executives took the energy company from blue chip to cow chip by using deceptive accounting practices throughout the 1990s to inflate the company's value. And Arthur Andersen, at the time one of the world's top five accounting firms, was dissolved as a result of its involvement in the scandal. Thousands of people lost their jobs and their pensions, and the fallout also led to the investigations into accounting practices (and the demise) of other companies like WorldCom and HealthSouth.

These scandals resulted from leaders failing to lead themselves. They read too many books about leading others and they mastered that black magic.

But they never dealt with the potential blackness lurking inside their own soul, the potential blackness that lurks inside each one of us.

"A MAN WHO WANTS TO LEAD
THE ORCHESTRA MUST TURN
HIS BACK ON THE CROWD."
–MAX LUCADO

The challenges to our moral fiber typically fall into one of five categories—greed, lust, revenge, independence, and pride—and all five require a somewhat counterintuitive response if we're to keep them from infecting our organizations like cancer. (I have a separate book that details these five challenges in more detail—*Five Storms in the Heart of Every Leader.*)

Greed: The temptation to have and hold more and more stuff that we don't really need. Antidote: We must open our hands and release what we "own." Rather than clutching more tightly to the "stuff" of life, we must give.

Lust: The temptation to wander with emotional and physical activity outside our covenant with God and/or our spouse. Antidote: We must take ourselves out of potentially tempting situations. We can't "manage" our level of dangerous involvement. We have to evacuate.

Revenge: The temptation to settle the score or balance the injustice done to us. Antidote: We must stand still. We can't retaliate and strike back. We have to trust justice to a higher authority. We must forgive.

Independence: The temptation to fly solo; the feeling that no one can really identify with our world and that we are all alone in sorting and navigating life. Antidote: We must "lean in" to someone else with transparency and vulnerability. We must engage others.

Pride: The temptation to think we're the sole cause and source of success, significance, and security. Antidote: We must promote others. Instead of sliding into self-focus, we discipline ourselves to shift our attention and energies to others.

Most leaders face all five of those temptations at some

point in our lives, and how we react impacts everyone around us. So we have to lead ourselves before we can safely lead others. The wisest man of all time, Solomon, in his Book of Proverbs, advised readers to learn from the ant that drives itself even though "it has no commander." It needs no constant cheerleading from those around it to get out and gather food before the harsh winds of winter kill all nutrition above the ground. It leads and manages itself.

Where do you need to push yourself? Where have you indulged inner moral laziness? A leader who does not hold himself to a high standard on inner character before he takes the lead risks becoming a lemming.

LEADING OTHERS AND MANAGING YOURSELF

☑ TRUE ☐ FALSE

LEADING OTHERS

☐ ☐   I clearly communicate my expectations to those I lead.

☐ ☐   I am available to those under my leadership when they need guidance or resources.

☐ ☐   I motivate and inspire the people I lead.

☐ ☐   Monitoring progress and giving feedback is enjoyable for me.

☐ ☐   I am known for giving people room to grow and develop under my leadership.

MANAGING YOURSELF

☐ ☐   Staying healthy mentally, emotionally, and physically is a priority for me.

☐ ☐   I have strong, life-giving relationships around me.

☐ ☐   I model the things I preach to others, especially the little things.

☐ ☐   I work hard to maintain integrity in the details of my daily work.

☐ ☐   I keep an updated self-development and growth plan in front of me.

CHAPTER 9

LIVING IN TRUTH

Feeling Confident **AND**
Being Humble

BASKETBALL FANS AT the University of Arkansas celebrate their home victories by singing a slightly altered version of the 1980 Mac Davis song, "Oh, Lord, it's Hard to be Humble." The players and cheerleaders go into the student section of Walton Arena, lock arms, sway left and right, and sing along with the music from the school's band.

"Oh Lord, it's hard to be humble
when you're perfect in every way.
I can't wait to look in the mirror
I get better looking each day.
To know me is to love me
I must be one hell of a fan.
Oh Lord, it's hard to be humble
When you're an Arkansas Razorbacks fan."

Ironically, Davis wrote the original version of that song early one morning when he found himself all alone. As the headlining act for a popular nightclub, he got to sleep in one of the nicest suites in a top-flight hotel. He had written hit records for Elvis, hosted his own television show, topped the charts as a country singer, and earned top billing as a live performer. But there he was, alone in his fancy hotel suite with nothing to keep him company but his guitar and his sense of humor.

Humility is no joke for those of us in the business community, though. If we go long enough without humility, life finds a way of delivering a big batch of it to our doorsteps. If we wallow in it, however, we'll never leave our front yard. So one of the greatest challenges leaders face is striking that balance between *humility* and *confidence*.

A leader without confidence simply isn't a leader. Action always flows from self-assurance. There is nothing wrong with knowing what you are good at and moving forward without

"IF WE GO LONG ENOUGH WITHOUT HUMILITY, LIFE FINDS A WAY OF DELIVERING A BIG BATCH OF IT TO OUR DOORSTEPS."

apology to make it happen. That is what leaders do. But an overdose of self-confidence always ends up smelling rotten. *You* might not smell it, but others will. And they eventually react to it in some unpleasant ways.

Humility doesn't mean that you dismiss your strengths. It simply means that you realize you aren't the sum total of the formula for success. Any formula for success includes other people, favorable circumstances and, usually, a pinch of luck.

Humility is the genuine adoption of that mindset.

Being confident means accepting who you are and doing what you know needs to be done. Being humble means recognizing what you aren't, accepting who others are and showing a willingness to enlist their help. Confidence does not mean omni-competence, and humility does not mean self-flagellation. Being confident means having the boldness to move forward when you are strong in a certain area. Being humble means admitting your shortcomings and asking the help of others whose strengths complement your weaknesses. Together they create the alloy for a potent leader.

The Apostle Paul was a hard-driving leader who did not slow down to pander to anyone, yet he had the broader wisdom to admit the importance to "not think of yourself more highly than you ought, but rather think of yourself with sober judgment." [5]

Sober judgment. Healthy self-awareness. That kind of balanced self-assessment is what it means to be confident and humble at the same time. In fact, you could make a case that true humility embodies honest confidence. To be truly humble is to understand the truth about yourself, the truth about others, and the truth about your situation. To accomplish this presupposes that you approach each of these with a certain level of confidence.

As you travel down the pathway to wholeness as a leader there is, perhaps, no greater combination that will affect those you seek to lead. An overconfident jerk of a leader will not engender trust in followers. But a leader who operates from a position of honest humility—in both work life and private life—is a leader others *want* to follow. The humble leader is an effective leader.

FEELING CONFIDENT *AND* BEING HUMBLE

☑TRUE ☐FALSE

FEELING CONFIDENT

☐ ☐   I know my strengths and believe in my leadership abilities.

☐ ☐   I do not shy away from resolving conflict on my team.

☐ ☐   I rarely get intimidated with powerful people, complex situations, opposing opinions, or criticism, etc.

☐ ☐   I feel that I am well suited for my job.

☐ ☐   When the game is on the line, I want the ball.

BEING HUMBLE

☐ ☐   I welcome and respond positively to new ideas from my team.

☐ ☐   I am hungry for and accept feedback.

☐ ☐   I show integrity and honesty in business and personal dealings.

☐ ☐   I often realize how much I don't know and haven't experienced.

☐ ☐   My success has as much to do with circumstances and things out of my control as it does with things I have orchestrated and achieved.

CHAPTER 10

THE LONE RANGER STILL NEEDS TONTO

*Embracing Team **AND**
Performing Alone*

IN THE SUMMER of 2004, America sent its "Dream Team" of the world's best basketball talent to the Olympics in Athens, Greece, for the much-heralded return of the Olympiad to its motherland. The Dream Team, however, proved a poor advertisement for the pure virtue of sporting excellence that the Olympic Rings symbolize.

Americans had only lost two men's basketball games in Olympic history. But in Athens, the U.S. lost three games and came home in shame with the ignominious booby prize of a bronze medal. The team's roster was the Who's Who in the world fraternity of Phi Slamma Jamma. They were all air and nothing but net. Unfortunately, they were also mostly prima donnas. They were not a team. Each was playing only for himself. Or at least that's the way it appeared. Perhaps they had never really learned to be team players.

Perhaps they had been coddled as "the talent" for so long that they had no appreciation for the team.

As they each put on their individual performances, their less-talented opponents played them like the Harlem Globetrotters. With the Americans distracted by their own center-court grandstanding, the underdogs pulled off the upset by simply playing as a team: They ran offensive plays that required some players to set screens or make passes in order to free up a scorer for an open shot. And they played "help" defense, communicating with each other about what was going on and helping teammates when they needed it. They proved that a sum is greater than its parts. The Americans never added up to a whole. Just working in a group does not make you a team.

What a difference four years later when the "Redeem Team" took another approach at the Beijing Olympics. Instead of a training camp that lasted three weeks, the team worked

> **"I AM REMINDED HOW HOLLOW THE LABEL OF LEADERSHIP SOMETIMES IS AND HOW HEROIC FOLLOWERSHIP CAN BE. — WARREN BENNIS. "**

together for three years. Instead of guaranteeing playing time or starting jobs, the players were told those decisions were up to the coach. Instead of focusing on one-on-one moves and dunks, they rediscovered the genius of team—which still led to plenty of dunks. With a new focus on complementing each other rather than seeking compliments for themselves, the American team rolled through the Games without a loss—and with gold medals around the players' necks. The most revealing statistical evidence?

In 2004, Stephon Marbury led the Americans with 3.4 assists per game, and no other player averaged more than 2.5.

In 2008, Chris Paul (4.1) and LeBron James (3.8) set the pace for a team that led the tournament in assists.

At the same time, there are situations when you have to deliver solo. Not everything is done as a team. Sure, the Chicago Bulls weren't a championship team in the NBA until they complemented Michael Jordan with the likes of Scottie Pippen and Dennis Rodman. But there were times when Jordan took the ball and dominated a game on his own. When the game was on the line, everyone knew who was going to get the ball. And players like Jordan put in hours and hours of work on their own to refine their skills.

Some work is attached to your calendar with just your name assigned to it—no one else's. For that you must have the discipline to carve out the energy and time to "just go get it done." No big party. No group effort. No mutual motivation. Just you and your assignment. Every successful athlete knows the loneliness of preparation and training. Every successful entrepreneur understands the self-discipline of getting up early and staying late to ensure a start-up's survival. Successful, sustainable leaders operate effectively on a team and efficiently on their own.

*EMBRACING TEAM **AND**
PERFORMING ALONE*

☑ TRUE ☐ FALSE

EMBRACING TEAM

☐ ☐   I share credit with the whole team.

☐ ☐   My team communicates well with each
other.

☐ ☐   I am deliberate about developing the
leaders around me, and I currently have a
strong bench.

☐ ☐   I will recruit others to join a project even
if all they bring is moral support.

☐ ☐   The most powerful competitive
advantage any company has is its high
performance teams.

PERFORMING ALONE

☐ ☐   I regularly take time alone to brainstorm and plan.

☐ ☐   I really don't like working alone and by myself.

☐ ☐   I can sort through all the things to be done, find the things with my name on them, and just go "get-'er-done." I don't need an external "pump-up" session.

☐ ☐   I find that most work is easier if you just do it yourself.

☐ ☐   Involving others usually slows things down or complicates things.

CONCLUSION

THE HERO
LEADER

CHAPTER 11

THE IMBALANCE
OF PEOPLE

*We're Hardwired to Yearn
for Wholeness*

WHAT IS A hero leader? Don't worry, I don't expect you to run out and buy a bat-suit or start wearing a Lone Ranger mask—although in the right context that could be fun. I'm also not trying to set a "superhero bar" for all of us to beat our collective leadership heads against.

A hero leader is someone who, like Batman, understands the need to possess more than one tool to get the job done. I just walked you through some paradoxical qualities that, if you take the time to hone them, will help you become a more effective leader. The difficulty lies in not becoming frustrated if they don't all come naturally to you.

By nature we are imbalanced people. After all, life itself is one big project of leveraging tension in order to achieve balance. And what is balance? Balancing is the act of utilizing counteractive weights. Some say we don't ever really balance anything. Rather, we learn how to live in the tension of imbalance.

On the tightrope that is balance, we naturally want to lean to one side, but we must train ourselves to lean a little bit to the other side. Otherwise, we will fall.

If we strip away all the leadership jargon and mumbo-jumbo, we see that these qualities we've just studied could apply to everyday life, and they are for anyone. In life, if I just focus on being a good father, my work will suffer. If I just focus on community work, because I have a natural proclivity toward it, my family will suffer. Each day I have the opportunity to wear several different hats: father, husband, professional, community leader, church parishioner, and so on. In order to keep it all together—to stay sane—I need to learn how to balance each facet of life. I must be the best professional I can be; but when I return home, I need to be fully present and fully dad.

And who doesn't want to be super-dad? I know I do.

We learned from Malcolm Gladwell that an *outlier* is a person who spends 10,000 hours honing a specific craft. We learned from Marcus Buckingham that each person has core competencies and those should be our focus; we shouldn't bother with things we're not good at.

But when we begin focusing all of our energy on what we're the best at we are, in essence, stepping off the tight rope. How can we walk the tightrope of life if we only know how to lean left or right?

RECOVERING WHOLENESS

As I read through my seven collective qualities and reflected on what it means to be a complete leader, I couldn't shake the notion that these truths are for the everyman, the everywoman. To the individual I am saying, "We should recover a real spirit and value of the Renaissance person." I'm not suggesting we kill ourselves trying to be the next Leonardo da Vinci. But we can take steps toward developing the whole person.

The Renaissance ideal feels artful to me. It was a time when people understood an individual to possess innate intellectual and physical tools. In order to form those tools to the utmost, a broad knowledge base was demanded and sought. The musician or writer didn't simply socialize with folks of his own ilk. He or she was able to converse on broad topics while living confidently in the security of their specific skill set. But in today's culture there are accountants and there are literary types. Affinity groups are everything. Right?

Our modern move toward specialization creates silo-living and silo-leading. As individuals, say homeowners, for example, we no longer need to know much about anything to maintain

"IF YOU WANT TO BUILD A SHIP, DON'T DRUM UP THE MEN TO GATHER WOOD, DIVIDE THE WORK, AND GIVE ORDERS. INSTEAD, TEACH THEM TO YEARN FOR THE VAST AND ENDLESS SEA." —ANTOINE DE SAINT-EXUPÉRY

our homes. If the furnace clunks out, we call a heating and cooling specialist. If the dishwasher begins leaking all over the new hardwoods, we call a plumber. Hail damage? Call a roofer. You get the idea.

Sometimes this specialization can cause rifts. In the knowledge world of MBAs, Ph.D.s, MDs, and JDs, there can sometimes exist a disdain for those in the physical labor world—as if it requires no knowledge to repair a BMW engine. Thinkers aren't laborers and laborers shouldn't think. Our love of specialization, therefore, can lead to a fragmented culture. In his *New York Times* bestseller *Shop Class as Soulcraft: An Inquiry into the Value of Work*, author Matthew Crawford suggests that we (as a culture) would rather have a world devoid of psychological friction than interact with the world of machines. In other words, we like our autonomous existence and are content to let the mechanical dudes fix our stuff.

But we were not created to be autonomous. We were created to integrate ourselves into the lives of others. We are hardwired to fix things, to learn things, to challenge, to be involved in more than just one thing. Human wholeness doesn't mean that we bag our core competencies and attempt to be the perfect humanist. It means that we operate out from our core but we're always looking for ways to learn and to connect with other humans.

WHAT I'M NOT SAYING

I want to reiterate that I *do* believe in core competencies. I'm not saying we abandon leading from our strengths. I think every person possesses a certain allotment of strengths and I think that leaders, in particular, should lead from that core—but not *only* from that core.

Our core competencies as human beings and leaders should work as a hub from which we develop the skills that don't come naturally for us.

We should play to our strengths.

Consider the late Steve Jobs. Jobs experienced the breadth of the computer industry like no other. He possessed a creative eye for product design and was an adept marketer. He was responsible for revitalizing a fiscally anemic Apple Computers, Inc. Some people regard Apple's turnaround as the greatest in business history. Today, Apple is the world's most valuable traded company. When I think of Jobs I think of him on a stage, an audience waiting with bated breath as the magician in the black turtleneck and jeans unveils another game-changer. He was a brilliant marketer.

But he wasn't known to be a stellar CEO in terms of leadership. Former employees regarded him as temperamental and overly perfectionistic. He would change his mind at a moment's notice.

But we don't look to Jobs for leadership advice per se. We look to Jobs for vision and innovation. He played to those strengths. That's not to say he didn't work on the things he struggled in. Some say the egomaniac Jobs was replaced by calmer, more patient Jobs. He knew what he did best and he did it to his utmost. But he never washed his hands of the qualities he possessed little competence in.

I'm no Steve Jobs. Who is? But I do recognize my core competencies and play to them on a daily basis. But I also love to expand my horizons.

On a professional level, I love to unravel and reshape a strategic mess. But just because I am naturally drawn to the macro strategic issues doesn't mean I can ever forsake the details of managing the day-to-day of my business. I'll never

"...WE WERE NOT CREATED
TO BE AUTONOMOUS.
WE WERE CREATED TO
INTEGRATE OURSELVES
INTO THE LIVES
OF OTHERS."

abandon what I'm best at, but I'll also never stop stretching myself so that I can learn more.

On a personal level, I love river and stream fishing. I'll probably never hit professional guide status, but that doesn't keep me from pursuing knee-deep rivers to stand in or float with my Jackson Coosa Kayak. And being skilled and knowledgeable to some level doesn't excuse me from ongoing learning and development.

At times I think we've lost the spirit of adventure when it comes to stepping out of our comfort zones and learning something new. We must always seek the next frontier in our professions and in life.

As individuals, we will live life to the fullest if we will simply apply ourselves to becoming well-rounded, whole humans. Likewise, in the professional world, we should play to our strengths but we should never abandon our weaknesses—i.e., outsourcing them to someone else. For leaders, this simply will not do.

CHAPTER 12

THE *NEW* EFFECTIVE

The End of One-Dimensional Competence

IT'S 1966. THE first *Star Trek* episode airs on television. Texas Western and its starting lineup of all-black players defeats all-white Kentucky for the NCAA basketball championship. Medicare is created by the federal government. Five hundred thousand American troops are fighting in Vietnam. A moderately well-known actor named Ronald Reagan becomes governor of California. A first-class stamp costs a nickel. The average home costs $14,200. The average American makes $6,900. And Peter Drucker publishes 200 pages on *The Effective Executive*.

As you know by now, I'm an out-of-the-closet Drucker fan. And I'm not alone. Over forty years later, leaders in every conceivable industry still refer to *The Effective Executive* as the best primer on leading and managing people and organizations.

Like so many of Drucker's insights, those contained in this book were far ahead of their time—creating both the language around an idea as well as a market to utilize the concept. You can count on Drucker for thoughts that outlast the latest marketing propped up, hot webinar topic.

In this case, I think Drucker was on to something simply with the title word, "effective." Not successful or satisfied. Not influential or intelligent. *Effective*. In chapter one I referenced this exact word because I think it holds the key to excellent leadership.

One definition of *effective* is "adequate to accomplish a purpose." But accomplishing a purpose is, at best, related to efficiency. That's a great job description for an executive—they need to possess adequate skills to accomplish something. But I prefer Drucker's definition of effectiveness: "Doing the right thing." Or, to put it another way, the effective leader is the whole leader—he or she understands that effective leadership comes from their ability to value the head *and* the heart *and* the hand.

The business climate has changed in the last forty years, but the need for effectiveness has not. We need whole leaders leading, not fragmented specialists.

In the preceding pages, we've looked at some of the qualities needed to be an effective executive. Let's close by looking at four stepping stones that will help you and I become the Modern Effective Executive.

MORE THAN ONE DIMENSIONAL

Stepping Stone One leads us to recognize that today's competitive market requires a leader to be more than one-dimensional.

I love the harsh realism of the commercial markets. It has a way of separating the professor of theory and the practitioner of reality. Or, as the old philosopher said, "A man with a testimony is never at the mercy of a man with an argument."

What I've learned from a quarter-century of working in the market myself and coaching scores of other market leaders is this: One-dimensional competence is not enough.

A hundred years ago, even forty years ago when Drucker was writing, we were in a specialization economy. The view was "know one skill and know it well." Find your spot on the assembly line and just get your hours in. Today, it's a knowledge world. You need a broad range of knowledge and the skill to apply it in a variety of different settings—with people, with tasks, meeting deadlines, outlining vision, and more. Every CEO I meet desperately needs leaders with a variety of skills.

The effective leader is thus the versatile leader. You wear several different hats and you have multiple plates spinning.

The effective leader has to have the ability to handle all of this, and more important, the wisdom to know which hat to wear at any given moment and which plate needs a helping hand. The head down, nose-to-the-grindstone leader just doesn't cut it anymore.

BE NATURAL, BE YOU

Stepping Stone Two walks us toward the realization that we need to appropriately use our built-in, internally engineered skills that just come naturally.

In all this talk of versatility, however, don't forget that you do have certain strengths. Each person is wired with skills that simply come naturally—logical thinking, relational intuition, steadiness, motivational skills, etc.

Take the time to identify the skills that come naturally to you. It can be as informal as a conversation with a boss or a friend that starts with, "What do you think my best skills are?" or as formal as taking one of the array of strengths inventory tests that are available. At the least, it will take some self-reflection. Then, once you've identified your built-in strengths, use them. Find a job or job responsibilities that utilize these special strengths. You'll be more satisfied and your company will be more profitable.

So, start with your strengths, but don't finish there. You can't afford to.

Books like Marcus Buckingham's *Now, Discover Your Strengths* are helpful to a point, but they often deny the reality that the modern market requires more than the four or five skills we're naturally good at. At some point, the market says, "You're not necessarily a long-range planner? Or, you think long range but not about today's to-do list? OK. Well, do it anyway or your effectiveness is limited."

YOU'RE NOT LEONARDO DA VINCI

Stepping Stone Three tells us to remember that none of us will ever be omni-competent.

Do you ever wish you could be all things to all people in your organization? Do you ever feel like you can do each task better than anyone else can? I hate to break it to you, but you can't. It's an illusion. And it's a false belief that causes tremendous stress for leaders (because they think it's all on them to figure out everything), and takes a tremendous toll on businesses (because their growth will only go as far as their struggling leader can go).

It's our culture that does it to us—everything we see and hear tells us about things we can have, things we can do, and secrets to solving our problems (imagine the slogan, "Just Don't Do It," or Bob the Builder's new catchphrase, "Can we fix it? No, we probably can't!").

Some of the marketing out there is good-intentioned, but as a whole, it gives the impression that we could do it all if we'd only buckle down or get the right advice. The reality, though, is that we could never do it all.

But *you* can do a lot. G.K. Chesterton said, "Art consists of limitation. The most beautiful part of each picture is the frame." In the same way, effective leaders figure out the skills that are most needed—the ones that must be in the frame—and they either have them or they get them. They don't worry about being omni-competent; they work to become multi-competent.

BROADEN YOUR HORIZON

Stepping Stone Four directs us to cultivate a broad portfolio of "developed and discovered" competencies.

In my hometown, there's a one-lane bridge called the Tilly

"IN THE END, IT IS IMPORTANT TO REMEMBER THAT WE CANNOT BECOME WHAT WE NEED TO BE, BY REMAINING WHAT WE ARE."
–MAX DEPREE, *LEADERSHIP IS AN ART*

Willy Bridge. On either side of the bridge (which is really more like a half-lane bridge) is the rushing water of a filled-to-the-brim ditch. Jerk the wheel to the right or to the left just a hair, and you're in the water. You have to stay in the middle of the lane.

That's the daily reality for the effective leader. On the left is the over-emphasizing of one's strengths and the neglecting of some of the real needs of the business. On the right is the omni-competence, trying to do everything. If you jerk the wheel to either side, you head straight into the creek, killing all progress while you wait for a rescue.

What I encourage leaders to do is to strive for excellence but to accept adequacy (not mediocrity). In the areas where you can excel (your built-in strengths), become one of the absolute best and center your core tasks around those skills. In the areas where you struggle and (let's be honest) never excel, work to get a passing grade.

My kid might excel at math, but he'd be thrilled with just a solid passing grade in history or art appreciation.

This balance is what I mean in talking about the levels of competence in Chapter 3. In all the key areas of our work, the effective leader must move to at least conscious competence. She might not be able to do certain tasks well without even concentrating, but she should get to the point where she can do each key area. Understanding that you need to be working toward conscious competence in your weaker areas along with flexing your "strong muscles" is the key to wholeness as a leader.

So where do you go from here?

You go to work.

You accept the fact that the executive specialist is dead, but that the opportunities for a modern effective executive are still present. And you figure out where you need to focus in order to increase your effectiveness, not just your efficiency.

The good news? If you want to become effective, you're in good company. Listen to Drucker one last time, speaking a half century ago:

"In forty-five years of work as a consultant with a large number of executives in a wide variety of organizations—large and small; businesses, government agencies, labor unions, hospitals, universities, community services; American, European, Latin American and Japanese—I have not come across a single 'natural': an executive who was born effective. All the effective ones have had to learn to be effective."

I couldn't agree more.

NOTES

1. *Depree, Max. Leadership Is an Art, 2004.*
2. *"The Head Gardener," Lessons Learned. Harvard Business School Press, 2007.*
3. *Drucker, Peter. Management Challenges for the 21st Century, 1999.*
4. *http://abcnews.go.com/Primetime/Story?id=1872255&page=4*
5. *Romans 12:3, NIV*

Steve is the founder of Coaching by Cornerstone, where he advises executives, business owners, and young entrepreneurs. When he isn't working his day job (or fishing), Steve writes and speaks often on topics related to strategy, work, and faith. After publishing the *Life@Work Magazine* some years ago, Steve recently launched a new writing and publishing venture, *stephenrgraves.com*. Through this venture, Steve is helping to stage conversations and create content around four themes he is passionate about: organizational strategy, social innovation, leadership development, and practical faith. To learn more, check out his weekly blog and look for the next book coming out soon.

For more resources from KJK Inc. Publishing, go to *stephenrgraves.com*.

Other titles from Stephen R. Graves:

Notes